IN MAGIKAL WATERS

poems by

Ruth Moon Kempher

Finishing Line Press
Georgetown, Kentucky

IN MAGIKAL WATERS

Copyright © 2017 by Ruth Moon Kempher
ISBN 978-1-63534-102-7 First Edition
All rights reserved under International and Pan-American Copyright Conventions.
No part of this book may be reproduced in any manner whatsoever without written permission from the publisher, except in the case of brief quotations embodied in critical articles and reviews.

ACKNOWLEDGMENTS

For their first use of my work collected here, and their implicit permission to reprint it, I would like to thank the editors of the following periodical publications:

Abbey, for "Looking for Ulysses," and "After Paul Klee. . ."
Chiron Review, for "Of Friezes. . ." "Adrift Near Canakkale, Cassandra Considers," "Captain's Table," "P. O. V.," and "Detritus [Trash] Poem, at Home"
Confrontation, for "Excursions: The Schedule…"
Exit 13, "Questionable Itinerary," "Boredom at Its Best," and an early version of "Of Gardens. . ." published as "Hidden Gardens"
Edgz, for "Listening for Lacunae"
Hanging Loose, for "Before Embarking. . ."
Hiram Poetry Review, for "Why the Fire Wept" [here, "Night Thought"]
Many Mountains Moving, for "Offshore Postcard: Aeolian Islands"
Minotaur, for "Routine #38674: Where Was I?"
Off the Coast, for "Specific Gravity: Gozo and Calypso"
Pearl, for "A Curious Aside"
Tiger's Eye, for "In Priam's Palace"

Publisher: Leah Maines
Editor: Christen Kincaid
Cover Art: Cover ad for Travel Dynamics International, New York City NY, for "Journey of Odysseus: Retracing The Odyssey through the Ancient Mediterranean," October 7-21, 2004.
Author Photo: Karen Moon Watts
Cover Design: Elizabeth Maines

Printed in the USA on acid-free paper.
Order online: www.finishinglinepress.com
also available on amazon.com

Author inquiries and mail orders:
Finishing Line Press
P. O. Box 1626
Georgetown, Kentucky 40324
U. S. A.

Table of Contents

Of Friezes I've Seen... 1
Routine #12334: Another Overture... 2
Adrift Near Canakkale, Cassandra Considers 3
In Priam's Parlor— 4
Excursions: The Schedule, After Averno 5
Cassandra, Who Knows Her Place.. 6
Captain's Table (Recalled) 7
Passageway Encounter 8
Specific Gravity: Gozo and Calypso 9
Before Embarking, There's.. 11
The Swimmer 13
A Curious Aside 14
Routine #38674: Where Was I? 15
Listening for *Lacunae*.. 16
Offshore Postcard: Aeolian Islands 18
P. O. V. 19
Night Thought: Why the Fire Wept 20
Looking for Ulysses 22
Questionable Itinerary... 23
Of Certain Labyrinths 24
Boredom at Its Best 25
The Purse 26
Routine #61315: Taking the Part 28
Of Gardens, Lately Seen... 29
After Paul Klee: "Temple Gardens" 30
Detritus [Trash] Poem, at Home 31

INVOCATION—

*Tell me, muse, of the man of many resources
who wandered far and wide after he sacked the holy
city of Troy...*
                    —Homer, *The Odyssey,* Book One

     Stately, plump
Kalliope, armed with cantos
loud enough to deafen, my vacuum beckons—
timeless cycles, bringing mnemonic, freighted
visions—
          Apeneck Sweeney
lost in the Tradewinds' dankness
questions glass-eyed Sibyllan images, mirrored
visages (April being past remonstrance)
bottle by bottle—
broods, particulate—that daft, musing beggar
darkly seeking. Strangely, I too have sought them:
foreign beaches, lovers, motel keys, bedrooms
better forgotten. . . .

OF FRIEZES I'VE SEEN
(on the Mediterranean)

I'VE
NOTICED

in the otherwise empty dining-
hall of Napoleon's house
on Elba—yellow
stucco walls
     and up high
all around, a line
of fat, flying, faded blue
bees, noble symbols—

later
in Pompeii—
satyrs.

ROUTINE #12334: ANOTHER OVERTURE, ANOTHER SHOW

"It's the secret Greek in me," giggles Cassandra oddly like a schoolgirl, licking her lips, unhinged like that time in the caves at Stonehenge, with the sun lost behind her. "O, to lie with the enemy's my passion, and I do wish—but travel being what it is, these days one settles for visions. . . and this is not the grocery list I intended. Meanwhile, the sun has risen austerely, over mouldering silent fountains. They have always searched baggage, looking for the gods know what, but taking my shoes off is absolutely the limit. O, all my Big Brothers, lost in the rubble of burnt bridges and fallen towers. . .where was I?

    hectic prophesies not withstanding, we'll need dog food. Sugar. Toilet paper. One year's list slides ineluctable into another, just so. . ." She's nodding off, whispers to herself since no one listening would believe her: "I mistrust these new translations, runes, inscriptions— 'Sermons in stones,' he said, but stones hold their secrets, though I can see right through to them, rainbow-ridden, prisms of dust, arisen."

ADRIFT NEAR CANAKKALE, CASSANDRA CONSIDERS

                     how odd—
after all the disasters, there's a certain
repetition that shows up, a motif: down a long hall
always there's a drift, voices of explanation—
numbers of victims, sad approximations
with no definitive answers—

    there'll be an old woman with her broom
or even herself, with a vacuum, attacking rugs
feverish to accomplish any half-way useful
or idiotic something at least, to keep
the mind elsewhere—

always listening, half an ear cocked
             to lives ticked off
someone sweeps up the dust
One tends to confuse disasters: which war
or volcano or tornado left the singular victim
                 sprawled, fingertips
on the vault wall—odd how each long hall
deep in shadow, one light left, candle
glow at the open door, allows
a murmur, apologetic
and unsure.

IN PRIAM'S PARLOR—
SECRETS OF THE PEACOCK'S BEADED EYE

> Heinrich Schliemann unearthed seven cities,
> one atop the other: times lines graphed them
> layer by layer.
> Mark Doty, "A Replica of the Parthenon"

1. Vision: cuneiform   petaled   upper of arras
prism   fans above delicate feathers   a precision
over the violent gold flair of tail   a violet triangle
beautiful with repetitious minor eyes   reflecting
easy evil present   mistaking the whorled disguise
flickers coiled in sleek pattern for the sensate oval

2. Motion: perhaps a passage of small breeze
presents inversion of life   scaled in the small eye
a return impaled on nails of mirror   all the past
alive   curled back in terror   embroidered threads
of forgotten needles capture   held fast forever
an antique dreaming   bird of royalty   survives

3.   Omens: pearls from the seabed rust flaked
slip from the beak   an open maw   fine teeth
a breathing of digressions   hints of lust
but the eye strikes heartmeat   fastens deep as any
talon   this simple trap   where eons pass
collapse   fracture   caught by the eyelid's beat.

EXCURSIONS: The Schedule, after Averno

        Today was Troy. Probably The Site
        or possibly a madman's obsession. Fits
5 o'clock somewhere over the yardarm
the 109 year-old veteran drank only
scotch and water until he died
            5:05 in the Palace of Circe, bristles
           embellish the captive's cheeks

rocks and dust, that was Troy
stones set in the hillside, a Turkish delight—was that Halvah?
honey and sesame and fifty photos later
        the huge Smyrna fig tree
        dust on furze leaves

these are the heroes who died
defending Priam and his
sons, the bastards
           back to the ship in time (5:25)
           for a Roy Roy, an olive

of course there were olive trees ubiquitous
clasping the cliff-sides, gnarled fingers
in the Mediterranean, the Aegean
        a drop in the Aegean
        that was Icarus

becoming a bird was popular (See Scylla.)
Saturday's saved for the Sibyl at Cuma. In her bottle, I believe.

CASSANDRA, WHO KNOWS HER PLACE GIRDS HER LOINS, FOR DINNER

below the salt, as usual, although on occasion
she's been elevated, for her wit's sake. . .

vastly aware how her hem drapes
crooked—leans to escape
foreknowledge, seeing

she's about to tip over into the fruit plate, into
an anguish of guava, mango and melon

looks at the mirror image: needs and hungers—
sees her fingers, predictable, gripped
tight against sure disaster.

She'll be the Fool again, but prays
secure in trust, for such
much is forgiven.

CAPTAIN'S TABLE (RECALLED)

    Served fettuccini, piles
of it, long eel-like pasta—
the menu calls it *pesca del mare*
(with fish of the sea)—it's rich with
tiny shrimps and buttery scallops
succulent, swaddled in noodles
with black-shell mussels, peeping
bringing memories of another
feast, blackest shells ever seen.
    The man from Michigan
at my shoulder has rack of lamb, with
ah, redolent rosemary, which is
not "rose" of the sea, but "dew"
of the sea—a sprig stuck up
curling petals, mini-tree—
I'd tell him but
    I'm distracted
an orchestra plays the opening bars
of "Moon River," and stops
abruptly and I can't interrupt his
tale of working out, arthritis
his loud laugh
    When was I at Cuma?
    When Taormina, looking
    for D.H. Lawrence?

When did I see the blue
    bees on Napoleon's walls
    that house on Elba?

what I really want to do is pinch his
rosemary, herb of remembrance:
that thirst, that greed.

PASSAGEWAY ENCOUNTER

Cassandra's voice ebbs, thin
and her sight's mistakes
more frequent, as well-known
creatures from her past impinge
across new faces, so she's
caught, calling the wrong name:

this steward's a Philippine
Carlos, clearly labeled on the
shirt-pin, yes, Carlos—
soft dusky skin like Odysseus—
trying to tell young Carlos, O
Odysseus, sometimes known as
Ulysses, don't let them tell you
you can't go home again.

SPECIFIC GRAVITY: GOZO & CALYPSO

there's this, a vague glimpse
on the ferry to Gozo—
aquamarine, glinting silver
water underfoot, and dripping
off railings, how it always is

On the survey form
I list myself MS, and wish
for a blank where I could
explain further—divorced, yes
but after twenty-one years
(we grew up together)
and he's died, but I'm not
a widow—it took so long to tan
the finger, where the ring was—

Later, how one's feet are gripped
as if the sand beneath was
a living, voracious creature;
red sand, an ugly beach
endless, to cross
finally, up high cliffs

The Guide says we're overlooking
Ramla Bay, from high on Gozo
"You have just retraced
Odysseus' footsteps and this—"

pointing at a breach in
tumbled, huge rocks—"This
is the entrance to his cave
where she kept him
seven years."

Think of it. Seven years a slave
seven years of daily visits
from the old hag, walks on that beach
he couldn't sail away from. . .
the air musty with brine

steps down into darkness, tip down
as I shudder, holding my breath
and here, a rope rail prickles
Seven. How it must have seemed
An eternity. Yet I won't deny
I gave three times seven, with
no idea how old lusts held me
nor how lost, that life.

BEFORE EMBARKING, THERE'S TOO LONG A WAIT

You have to sit, be patient
listen to the string of wives
bitching at their husbands, I

wouldn't use that tone to dogs—
cats or snakes, maybe, pigeons—
all helpless critters shrivel, die

when badly used too often.
Such derision. Hateful women.
Why are there so many, cruising?

In long moments like those
lately, I think of Jonah, the ex-
husband, now deceased, sadly—

Juana la Loca, who carted
the corpse of her Prince every-
where with her, had nothing on me—

as I travel alone, he's here, voice
in my ear, he reminds me it's
Curacao he liked, it was

St. Martin he hated, when his ship
the *Pilau* went there, and I would
see Curacao, in spite of the wives—

from the railing, I'd seen colors—
a flapping bazaar of veils or banners—
where did navy ships anchor there?

He's disgusted at my ignorance.
They had to anchor out, were
motored in by tender, of course.

THE SWIMMER—

         Icarus
not brainy, but greatly
muscled—having flown
         on wax wings
too high, dropped
(the poets say) unnoticed—
plummeted somewhere
convenient, off Corfu
into heaving waters.
         Like (much
later) Prospero
drawn on by the island's
twangling music
         Icarus
kicked free of his molten
harness, long hair swaying
under water like
         seaweed
no longer crisped victim, but
now voyager, surviving
with backstrokes plus
         flotation
found the black witch—
Caliban's blue-eyed mother—
waiting for him on the beach.

A CURIOUS ASIDE

Haven't I always tried to switch
    Cypress and Crete? it's the C's

        odd, I'm so often confused—
it's the Cassandra in me, I believe

    still, there was
a man from Cypress whose smile was

      sudden, the lower lip pushed out
    but I wasn't certain—

and O, the islands I loved, raw cliffs
and harsh beaches, in azure seas—

      dolphins and deities
    something drew me, always

to the warmth, the sun in people
    and yes, yes

        it was always so, even
    in the incredible knowing—
what slips away, is memory.

ROUTINE #38674: WHERE WAS I?

Proteus preserve us, it was Cassandra I thought I was, but have I spent my whole life lost and confused in the lives of others? This is a Henny Youngman script, with music by Shirley Sinatra or Piaf, the menu by the Marx Brothers, Karl and Harpo. When my Greek hairdresser told me the ship I was on was only two years in service, and I'd swear I was on it at least ten ago, but then this did seem bigger, but I thought in my heart they'd euchred me with a Daedalus-like apparition, a wonder of science and reconstruction. But I was that tired, from the mobs at the gates and all the flung luggage, I had to accept her story. My ship known in the past was sold at auction, and what pray tell did they do with Odysseus? It was James Joyce back then, told me, Listen Baby, and of course I've lost it. Believe me, it wasn't Henny but Herman Melville whispering in my ear, something evil lurks always slyly around the corner, when you deal with masquerade.

LISTENING FOR *LACUNAE*

              at Cuma
on a grey day, the Sibyl of course
wasn't home. The high stone walls
around us were Roman, not
Greek, as the fat pedant
traveling professor
insisted; nor
      was I surprised. The hole
into which the Oracle spoke
was knee-high—a pipe-line—
the grouchy jackass assured us
sending a skillion years of tourism
blithely down the drain—water storage
for Roman (not Apollo's) troops.
      This ancient holy tunneled cave
sits just off the two-laned macadam
from grim Lake Avernus—Virgil's
entrance to Hades—where even
today, birds sing.

Volcanic steams no longer
hiss, but linger lethal, as toxic
as the breath of the pedant
yammering "Not Greek.
 Roman."
The Sibyl's silent: that Priestess
long ago faded into her bottle
but soft in the small breeze
as the tour, sad unbelievers, moves on

there's chanting: "*Hic, haec, hoc*
 hius
  hius..." It's
Miss Cory from Fourth Year Latin.
She's declining. Behind me
our Guide's small dog
cocks his ears—
agrees.

OFFSHORE POSTCARD: AEOLIAN ISLANDS

> *Where we are is anyone's guess. The*
> *gates to nowhere multiply and the present is*
> *so far away, so deeply far away.*
>
> Mark Strand, "Bury Your Face in Your Hands"

Laid along the haze of shore are the usual Mediterranean houses like building blocks, white with black (possibly obsidian) window-spaces. At breakfast, a man named Schwartz was telling me obsidian was mined here, and to look for artifacts, cheap. Ochre archways hang there, higher on the hillside, where one church wall catches sunlight in Moorish curves. Its steeple clanks, calling for attention, tinny. A hydrofoil ferry, the *Giovanni Bellini*, glides by pale blue, with a whirl of sonar blades—it's from Palermo. It's altogether too peaceful. The Wind God, Resident, Inhabitant (that's the Guide's description) lurks somewhere in a cavern—thinking up new sport, new tricks. Someone whistles. The eye of a serpent, unblinking, is seen obsidian, somewhere in a poem.

P.O.V.—
> *Out of Time. All of these things are exceedingly old—*
> *the sketch, and the ship, and the afternoon.*
>   Cavafy, "On the Ship"

       off the coast
of Santorini, I'm afloat
(on the moored ship) looking

       across azure ripples
to vast, high escarpments, a cliff
(volcano thrust) out of incredible water

       with toy white houses
and a white domed church, like icing
on a layered cake (except it's tiers of lava)

       where a white road-scar zips
up (where our bus went earlier, gasping)
making a Greco-Assyrian ziggurat. What

       I can't believe is that blonde
(bleached) yenta in the tender: her scowling:
"I'm from California and it all looks the same."

NIGHT THOUGHT: WHY THE FIRE WEPT

	Why the fire wept was not resin only
She looks at the	or so many good men dead
fire, thinking	or Dido's bones
of Luis dead	time lickering, the fire song
and now Duke died	a nasal tone through pine
and Joe James	So many tall ships broken to salt
last week, so	nests of lost gulls and tortoise
many good men	piled in their last home, moulder
gone	as driftwood burns sea blue and purple
	like the sky before storm
	Salt tears, dry
She thinks of you	She lay down in her own flame, aware
and knows somehow	how the fire moans
you live	so many good men dead
and remembers	so many women gone
your black darts	each ring's the record of a year
painted like sharks	*gymnospermae*, the scientific
and Luis was	how we go on, naming
no good at darts	the good growth, firm
except	and the musk growth, *fungi*, convolute forms
once a year	
New Year's he'd	
play	so be it. amen.
	She knew what she was doing
and fires	
he'd lay such fires	fire to fire, flesh to flame, lay down
at the Tavern	where flames lapped like water
cold days	flickered. He was gone
Z. bartending	and sense had fashioned
would say they'd	only the pyre
never catch	embers at dawn.

"One match" Luis   So many lifetimes lived in one lifetime
would say. "I'm   multiple exposure of ourselves
a warlock. . ."   and others
and wave his   in various poses, known
wrist, just so   illustrations for a ripped book
                          thrown to a fire, only
& how the fire   the lush ash falls in piles
blazed   lines linger
the glow   as if the ink or something
of his face &   were impervious to flames
even higher   words, looped like fishline
devilish   of the lightest test
glare of it   hovered somewhere, nylon
glazed   or meld with groove lines of the brain
in owl eyes   stayed, like veins in the granite of earth
eyes of those   or dust of granite, suspended in rain.
andirons
made by
his
father
                          So be it: amen

                          I turn and return to the fire
                          some chill lodged in my bones remains
                          The fire that warms me though
                          is not so warm
                          as the memory of your hands.

LOOKING FOR ULYSSES

    we landed at his homeport, on Ithika
    a grey-green bump in those incredible
    magical azure waters—what we found
        was a goat.
    Its tin bell clinked and I looked up
    the stone crop side of the mountain—
    silly goat hung out perilous, jaw in motion
    gnashing its lunch, whatever
    passes for lunch in the island's goat-world—
    noticed the silence, after its bell sounded
    maybe the birds were frightened.
    In these islands, the gods had a habit
        of turning girls into birds
    more for their safety than songs, but
    there were long lines of olive trees, silver
    spread sleeping beside and beneath us
        in bright glare of sun, a song
    would have broken the spell.
    Ulysses unfound, the goat
    enough, we sail home.

QUESTIONABLE ITINERARY: SIDE TRIP TO TUNIS

> *Was Troy lost for a kiss,*
> *or a run of notes on a lyre?*
> H.D., *Helen in Egypt*

they are getting rid of dictators
right and left, all around Tunis—
rioting in the streets of Egypt—
burning mosques in Libya
not to mention tourists—there
where Tunisia sticks up
on Hannibal's Africa, his desert
complete with elephants
like a sore thumb on the globe.

But I had a thirst, and tickets
to see Tunis, which was once
Carthage. On my list: visit
the site of Dido's suicide pyre—
where flames licked, lusty
    for unrequited love;
smolder yet, for the unjust.

OF CERTAIN LABYRINTHS
and of webs.

To Umberto Eco, a classical labyrinth
is Ariadne's thread, and conjecture's space
is a rhizome; connecting rhizomes make a maze.

Ourselves duplicitous, amazed, we wander
where boxwoods hedge together—It's a privet
mystery—how the dark leaves dangle

and whisper together. O, if they knew
the heat of your fingers—if they were suspicious. . .
those faceless watchers, surprised. . . .

In the middle of a myth about spiders
sits Miss Muffet—a child-faced Minotaur
smack on her tuffet—sits and cackles as her pet

arachnid spits raddled webs for us to follow.
I wouldn't do THAT, for words. I've seen
what happens. Continual mistakes. Lost hopes—

Ariadne, left high and dry at Naxos—
it's a nightmare. The hedges swarm
with mites and those famous curds are alive

with crawly maggots. It's exhausting:
I play the moppet and you play the spider.
I play the eternal seeker after day's lost light.

BOREDOM AT ITS BEST: NOTES OFF MONACO

> *Color possesses me. I don't have to pursue it.*
> Paul Klee, Diaries 4/16/14 in Tunis

trying to be blasé, with the Sultan's yacht bobbling
at portside, its oil magnet owner rents it
what? six thousand a day? peanuts.

heading for Tunis tomorrow, I do my daily
reading in the *Diaries* of artist Paul Klee
who left for Tunis from Provence

in when? 19-something. I should look—
what's important is, long ago, he came here
as a young man, seeking clarity and color. He says.

His favorite was orange. Sunset over stucco.
Is that why I came? People have asked me, why
to Tunis? Is it because I read about it, in Paul Klee?
or is it rather that Tunis is the site of Ancient Carthage
I always said I'd like to visit, reading Virgil's *Aeneid*—

some folks understand that: others are happier
with the artist. Some, dumbfounded, either way.

THE PURSE

I carry was new
as of Corfu—
purchased in a shop
on a long lane of
purse shops—
dusty, and smelling
faintly of abattoir
and no, I chose
not to dicker—

someone said last
night at dinner
you must always
refuse the first
offer (also spoke
of Greek mendacity
in all dealings) but
I do not haggle

I was in truth, still
bemused by a line
from Lawrence
Durrell's *Prospero's
Cell*, telling tales of
Caliban's mother—
that mysterious blue-
eyed hag, owner of
the island (Corfu)
upon which
Prospero was cast...

I do like the bag.

The merchant was
aghast, that I wouldn't
(that word 'hag' perhaps)
haggle. I'd not thought
much—'til reading the
Durrell book while eating
English breakfast: eggs
and kippers and muffins—
about Corfu having such
rich Shakespearean
connections.

The bag holds stuff
like a picnic hamper
if one needs one
or a home for a dog, but
the man in the shop
was so nonplussed
he sold it cheaper than
anyone expected.

I have always left
bargaining to my (brown-
eyed) mother, a shopping
maven who did enough
embarrassment to me
in John Wanamaker's
and Bonwit Teller's
years ago, far away.

ROUTINE #61315: TAKING THE PART

"Little routes," as Bubbsey Cappellia used to say, back in Trenton "veins," and we agreed in a locker room full of odors, it's a cockamamie world, it's webbed and rutted with spider thin wires, lines and it's worse today. In my flight through the rarefied clarity of a cloudless sky summing my travels up, I had in hand a new translation peculiarly apt, flying across an unseen ocean: having taken the part of Cassandra, I'd read her curse to not-be-believed was Apollo's gift, the spit of his farewell kiss, ephemeral and limited as any truth is—the new translator of Neruda's old world calls himself "accidental" as he writes of carrying across meaning in his search for kinship, comfort, everywhere finding "reminders of pain and death." O, yes. I climbed those terraced heights of Machu Picchu, inched upwards with my cane, weary and yet again: "disillusioned...disconnected from my people," taking the part of Dido— drawn to flame, the Incan altars at the mountain's green-swathed crest in that lost city our Guide insisted was never lost. It was cold. As I sat to find breath, I thought of my mother's slender hands back in Trenton patting my wet snowsuit, zipping me into everything.

OF GARDENS, LATELY SEEN

(on the Mediterranean, and elsewhere)   [To] *man, the garden should be something without and beyond nature, a gateway through which imagination lifted above the somber realities of life may pass into a world of dreams. . .easy enough if we were living in the age of Virgil the Enchanter. . .but. . .*
   Sir George Sitwell, On the Making of Gardens

I've noticed
while looking for something epic
and unchanged, like the engraving
   in *Latin IV—The Aeneid—*
sandy plains stretching, endlessly
undulant—camels.

   You can rent a camel
in Carthage today: and of Dido's
realm, only a small garden
graveyard remains—
ancient stones tilted just off
a busy street
   over a low wall
someone's barbecue
by a garage—our guide waves
at dusty grasses, speculates
animals or children
sacrificed

later
at home, geraniums
thirst in their pots
weeds flourish.
   In garden
places
a sense of peace.

AFTER PAUL KLEE: "Temple Gardens"

                      Adobe must be
what's grown here, or stucco, since
the only apparent greenery's a frond or two
stuck in sideways, very palm-suggestive—
                in all three panels (and I do
understand he scissored the original and re-
arranged the order of these three panels, but
I'm never quite sure when someone says "right,"
do they mean my right, looking at it? or their right
holding it up?) there are repetitive arch pieces
of that sun-baked orange, and a tower—
pathways with flat flagstones, grey-blue
and rust, burnt-orange. They say, in Tunis—
where he was enchanted by the light—
this was for him, "a turning point."

               Where the artist stands
is somewhere in the garden. The temple
is cranial, perhaps, an entirely mental
point of view, cured by scissors.

I dream his eyes mosaic: gleeful sun-gold
                    shining through.

DETRITUS [TRASH] POEM, AT HOME

On the ambit of an upper shelf
sit two small relics:
    the little pitcher, grey-blue sky
    with sheep scene, wool-white bodies
    sharply nosed grey heads and legs
    in a green tinge pasture: it sits
    beside a square tile, white
    with a deep blue jacketed, Greek man
        fishnet in hand
    apologizing to a big bird
    with red beak and flat feet
    who eyes him with suspicion.
In between the pitcher, from La Mancha
and the tile from Mikanos, lie years
of fallow manuscripts and grief.

    I added three stones from my pocket:
    One from Machu Picchu
    one from the walls of Troy, and
    one from the cave of the Cumean Sibyl.

    They tell me
    the Incas have vanished
    the Trojans were easily fooled
    and a dry wind speaks for the Sibyl.

Ruth Moon Kempher, an ex-navy brat, and ex-navy wife, was born in Red Bank, NJ in 1934, while her father was studying Classics at Rutgers. Her poetry and short prose—fiction and critical articles—have appeared in journals and other periodical publications since verse publications in the early 1960's, in *McCall's, The Saturday Evening Post, Bitterroot,* and *The Village Voice.* She is now retired from owning The White Lion Tavern in the historic San Agustin Antigua area of St. Augustine, Florida, and from twenty-five years of teaching in the English Departments, of first Flagler College, where she taught Creative Writing for her tuition, with a Florida Teacher's license based on her publications, and then, after obtaining her MA at Emory University, for twenty-one years for St. Johns River State College at various St. Augustine campuses. Since 1993, she has published the work of many poets through her Kings Estate Press, in single chapbooks and anthologies—collections which are always illustrated, including those of Gerald Locklin, Wayne Hogan, Hilary Tham, D. E. Steward and David Chorlton. She is also the author of *Always the Beautiful Answer: A Prose Poem Primer*, now in second printing. In 2012, her manuscript *What I Can Tell You* won the Bright Hill Press Poetry Book Award, and it was published in Spring, 2013. Another book-length collection, *Retrievals*, was released from Presa Press in June, 2015, and the chapbook, *The Skinny About J's Zinnias* was issued by Chiron Review Press in 2016.

www.ingramcontent.com/pod-product-compliance
Lightning Source LLC
LaVergne TN
LVHW041601070426
835507LV00011B/1237